DRYDEN AS AN ADAPTER OF SHAKESPEARE

AMS PRESS

NEW YORK

DRYDEN AS AN ADAPTER OF

SHAKESPEARE

BY
ALLARDYCE NICOLL, M.A.

THE DE LA MORE PRESS LTD. 10 CLIFFORD
STREET BOND STREET LONDON W.1

1922

Library of Congress Cataloging in Publication Data

Nicoll, Allardyce, 1894-
    Dryden as an adapter of Shakespeare.

    Reprint of the 1922 ed. published for the Shakespeare
Association by H. Milford, Oxford University Press,
London, which was issued as no. 8 of Shakespeare
Association papers.
    Bibliography: p.
1. Shakespeare, William, 1564-1616 — Adaptations.
2. Dryden, John, 1631-1700 — Criticism and interpretation.
3. Shakespeare, William, 1564-1616 — Adaptions — Bibliography.
I. Title.   II. Series: Shakespeare Association, London. Papers; no. 8.
PR2880.D7N5   1975   822.3'3   78-173083
ISBN 0-404-07848-6

This reprint has been authorized by the Oxford University Press

From the edition of 1922, London
First AMS edition published in 1975
Manufactured in the United States of America

AMS PRESS INC.
NEW YORK, N. Y.   10003

PREFATORY NOTE

SINCE the delivery of the following paper early in 1921 two volumes on Shakespeare adaptations have been published. One of these is the collection of altered plays edited by Mr. Montague Summers; the other is the careful work of Professor Odell, of Columbia University, entitled *Shakespeare from Betterton to Irving*. In his preface Mr. Summers has gathered together a mass of recondite and interesting information concerning players and the dates of production, and Professor Odell in the course of his chapter on the Restoration period has analysed with painstaking enthusiasm the actual scenic conventions which governed the stage in the time of Betterton. Hardly anything has been left to be done on his own particular line by either writer.

My excuse for printing the following paper is that I feel I have dealt with one or two aspects of these adaptations which have remained practically untouched by Mr. Summers and Professor Odell. I have printed it now, practically as it was delivered, and would draw attention to the fact that it was never intended, could never have been intended, to be in any way exhaustive. It was meant to serve merely as an introduction to a subject which in 1921 had been barely noticed by English scholars. I had intended then to issue it along with a reprint of the Dryden - D'Avenant *Tempest*, but in this latter task, pleasant yet laborious, I have been anticipated by Mr. Summers, who has included that long-forgotten version in his volume of adaptations. I have, however, added as an appendix a short bibliography of the chief alterations of Shakespeare issued between 1660 and 1700. This, again, is not intended to be complete, but merely outlines the main sources of information regarding this whole subject. I may note that many of the details given in the bibliography concerning performances of Shakespeare's plays and of adaptations are taken from documents which I have recently discovered in the Public Record Office.

DRYDEN AS AN ADAPTER OF SHAKESPEARE

THE study of the Restoration adaptations of Shakespeare, although at times it may appear a trifle depressing, is in reality one of the most interesting and the most profitable of all the fields of literary research. Neglected in the past, those adaptations, wretched and garbled renderings of Shakespeare's work though they may be, have a value all their own, a value which is becoming ever more and more apparent as we approach towards a greater and less biased interest in the theatre of the Restoration.

Our first duty, of course, in approaching such comparatively virgin ground as is presented to us here, is to look around and to discover under what aspects we may best and with most profit survey the country laid open before us. In doing so, we shall find that there are two distinct aspects under which we may regard at least such adaptations as date from 1600 to 1700, both of them important, the one leading back to Shakespeare himself and the other pointing to the new characteristics of a later age.

The first of these two aspects is the value which the Restoration adaptations may have for the text of Shakespeare itself.

In the year 1660 the dramatists were separated by not quite half a century from the latter years of Shakespeare's life, and consequently the altered plays which they produced, however badly mangled they might be, may have some interesting light to shed upon the text of the originals. There is just the possibility, though in many cases a faint one, that the dramatists of the Restoration, D'Avenant and Dryden in particular, may have had before them some quarto unknown to us, or even—a still more tempting thought—they may have had some MS. prompt-book in front of them when penning their plays. In some cases, of course, it is quite obvious that the ordinary folios were utilized as a basis, for example, in Dryden's *Troilus and Cressida*; but sometimes, as in the *King Lear* of Tate, we discover variations which point to no known original. We can hardly imagine Tate having before him several quartos and a folio or two in constructing his play, yet we find a number of the lines preserved in the quartos retained, a number missed out, and minor readings now from the quarto, now from the folio. D'Avenant's *Macbeth* presents just such another problem. In it are the songs of Middleton's *Witch*, and these, as Furness notes, are 'so highly fanciful, and come in so happily where D'Avenant has placed them, that one is almost tempted to believe that they were written by Shakespeare, and had been omitted in the printed copies of his play.' Here, undoubtedly, there is room for a great deal of detailed analysis.

Fascinating as this aspect of the Restoration adaptations is, however, it must be confessed that its tangible value is small when compared with that other aspect— the light which such adaptations throw on the spirit of the age in which they were produced. Shakespeare is a figure so colossal that he forms a kind of touchstone to any particular period, and we could almost write a history of English thought from 1623 to 1921 by studying alone the attitude displayed towards him by succeeding poets and critics.

We may say that the Restoration saw the first real adaptations of Shakespeare. Previous attempts there had been to better his works, but the period between Shakespeare's death in 1616 and the year 1642 had not nurtured so unbounding a self-confidence as was produced from the year 1660 onwards. The wits of the court of Charles II were nothing if not sure of themselves. They looked to France, certainly, for some inspiration, but they made no secret of their belief that they, after all, were superior to the French—even in art. Langbaine, in mentioning Lacy's *The Dumb Lady: or, The Farrier made Physician*, a rehashing of *Le Médecin malgré lui* and *L'Amour médecin*, declares that the plays of Molière have been much bettered in their English dress: and Shadwell, in his preface to *The Miser*, taken from *L'Avare*, modestly remarks that he 'may say without vanity, that *Molière's* part of it' had 'not suffer'd in' his hands, and goes on to remark that he had never known a '*French* Comedy made use of by the worst of our Poets, that was not better'd by 'em.' If that was their attitude towards the wit of Molière, what must we expect when we come to their attitude towards those rude barbarians of the age of Elizabeth who faultily set the English stage in such a shaky position that it had to be buttressed up with many additions ere it could be utilized for public performance? Cibber, in making *Wit at Several Weapons* into *The Rival Fools*, declared that he had chosen the 'unfinish'd hints' of these scenes from '*Fletcher's* loose confed'rate Muse,' and Richard Duke, in his laudatory verses prefixed to Dryden's *Troilus and Cressida*, announced gravely to his friend that he had found Shakespeare's play 'dirt,' he had left it gold. Similarly, Sir George Raynsford, in the prologue to Tate's *The Ingratitude of a Commonwealth*, very much altered from *Coriolanus*, after affirming that 'Shakespeare's "sacred Ghost" was appeased'—how he knew we cannot tell—informed the audience that the author 'only ventures to make Gold from Oar,

And turn to Money, what lay dead before.'

As a final example, and examples are well-nigh innumerable, we may note that Shadwell, in adapting *Timon of Athens*, printed his result with the title *Timon of Athens, the Man-Hater, Made into a Play*.

This infinite self-confidence is, I think, the first and primal characteristic of the age of Charles, and it explains the number of adaptations, not only from Shakespeare, but from Molière, Racine and de Vega, which supplied the two London theatres with much of their fare. The age was between the decadence of Elizabethan exuberance and the birth of classicism: it was not truly creative, but it craved for art: and it had no scruples about making up for its lack of creative power by filching and altering dramatic glories of the past.

It is not my place here, of course, to speak of the Restoration drama as a whole, but, as part of our object is to see Shakespeare reflected in an age, it may not be unfitting to sum up very briefly what seem to be a few of the main characteristics of the drama from 1660 to 1700.

We are naturally struck first of all by the growth of the heroic tragedy, and alongside of that of the witty and immoral comedy, now of low life, now of better-class manners. Both of these, at least in my opinion, may be traced, not to foreign or other imitation, but to the weakening, decadent fibre of the times. The age was essentially unheroic; but while it had not the courage in serious drama to throw over the inculcation of heroism and honor, it desired that there should be no nonsense about having to live up to heroic ideals. On the other hand, in comedy it did not object, nay it desired, to see an image of its own immoral, witty, elegant existence. The Restoration beau did not mind viewing himself as he was, nor did he mind viewing impossibilities of love and honor and goodness; what he objected to was seeing before him on the stage what he might have been. Here, then, is the fundamental explanation of the heroic species and of the manners' comedy. As the years advanced the former, becoming more and more idealistic and fanciful, degenerated into opera, and the latter, with the decaying spirit of the time, grew fouler and fouler, more and more farcical, year by year. From both points of view, Shakespeare's dramas were unacceptable to a people of this time. In comedy his real and simple, yet idealistic romance, and his early, often be it confessed crude, word-play, offended the sensibilities of dramatist and of audience alike. In a prologue written for a 1667 performance of James Shirley's *Love Tricks*, we are quite frankly told that

> That which the World call'd Wit in *Shakespeare's* age,
> Is laught at, as improper for our Stage.

In this connection, also, it is interesting to notice that in 1673 when Richard Ward, 'a Preacher of the Gospel in *Hartford*-shire,' as he called himself, was looking around for a quotation to illustrate the use of 'unprofitable, and ineffectual Words,' he chose some ten lines from *The Merchant of Venice* as a prime example. For once, the theologians and the dramatists were in complete accord; Shakespeare, they agreed unanimously, whatever else he could do, could not write decent English. In tragedy, too, Shakespeare was far too passionate and life-like. One might conceivably be a noble Macbeth lured to inglorious perdition : one might be an Othello in the harrowing toils of love and jealousy : no one possibly could have been an Almanzor who defeats whole armies of thousands of men single-handed.

The other characteristics of the Restoration stage all hinge upon the same debility in the temper of the people, and upon the reaction to that debility. Novelty was demanded at all costs, hence singing, dancing, impossible incidents throng the plays. The great outlook on humanity which had characterised the Elizabethan period was gone, and hence we find even the most noble dramas, such as *Venice Preserv'd*, instinct with petty political reference. The reaction is seen in the rapidly growing classical movement, which, although in England it never succeeded in driving out the romantic qualities inherent in our nationality, did give us our Augustan age with its *Cato* in the early eighteenth century. Finally, we must note that, keen and brilliant externally as this period was, it was not profound. Excesses had ruined its power of concentration and of thought. Its wit is sparkling, but superficial: its tragic dialogue often beautiful, but never deep.

On turning to the alterations made in the dramas of Shakespeare by the Restoration dramatists, then, it will not be amiss to divide such changes into several categories. Obviously the Restoration adaptations of Shakespeare differ one from another, and the reasons that led to their composition were not the same in every case. Roughly we may say that these changes naturally divide themselves into eight separate categories.

1. There were changes made because of a genuine critical dissatisfaction with Shakespeare's development of a scene or of a character.

2. There were changes due to the desire for making more heroic, elements already instinct with heroism.

3. There were changes made owing to the influence of the classic spirit.

4. There were changes made in comedy through the influence of the new spirit of wit and reckless immorality.

5. There were changes made in order to pander to the prevailing desire for novelty.

6. There were changes made in order to enforce a political parallel between Shakespeare's plot and contemporary conditions.

7. There were changes made for the purpose of simplifying Shakespeare's language.

8. And, finally, there were changes due to a thoughtless and senseless passion for any kind of alteration.

The changes due to the last cause are really fewer than might have been expected. In a few plays, indeed, we feel that the adapter has gone needlessly out of his way to change some minor phrase of Shakespeare's, for

left out, as a way of reasoning that will justifie killing any man, since there is nobody so inconsider(ab)all as some how or other has it not in his power to hurt his fellow. So in the place of it I would have Brutus conclude in this manner:

"If this be wrong ye Immortal Gods who read the Hearts of Men, Judge not the Action, but the Intent: Brutus might laugh whilst his sad country groaned, if Brutus was a Villain. Yet I am strongly tempted by the repeated sharp Complaints of Rome. Brutus, thou sleepest! Awak! And see thy selfe! Speak! Strike! Redress I will, but first I'll prove this hauty man and try if he'll be mov'd by Reason; if not, O Rome, I make thee promise, etc."'

'Here,' continues Killigrew, 'I wou'd have a scene betwixt Cæsar and Brutus upon the Ill Success of which Brutus shou'd take his resolutions . . .' Later on he tells us that he would leave out the famous 'Et tu, Brute'—'as it tends to reproach Brutus by the seeming tenderness of the Expressions, as if he could not have fell without him, but that when he rais'd his hand 'twas time for him to die. Besides the words of a dying man make strongest Impressions, and these last of Cesar's blacken Brutus with Ingrat(itude), which excites pity for the tyrant and Horror for the Patriot contrary to yᵉ design of yᵉ Author. Though it is very possible,' continues Killigrew, 'many understand the Beautys of Shakespeare better than me, yett I don't think it easy, Madam, for any body to admire 'em more. This is by way of preface to the following difficultys. I allways find whenever I read this Excellent play, I can't account for hating the Historicall Cesar and grieving for the Poetical one, for my aversion to slavery and yet following the cause of the tyrant with my best wishes through all the fortunes of Anthony and Octavius. This is a contradiction I can solve no way but from disliking the Patriots, whom I comprehend all under Brutus, for without him I question whether it would ever have been attempted—which at first sight seems to justifie Brutus, as (find)ing himself the only man able to free his Country. . . .'

Here, obviously, we have a reasoned piece of criticism allied to practical suggestions for the altering of the conduct of the piece. Unfortunately, we possess no rendering of *Julius Cæsar* which at all seems guided by Killigrew's proposals: the *Julius Cæsar* which I shall later mention being altered on quite a different plan.

Dryden's first adaptation of a play of Shakespeare's was *The Tempest: or, The Enchanted Island*, acted in 1667 and published in 1670 with a preface dated 1669. In 1674 a play with the same title, and containing Dryden's original preface, was printed, and this 1674 edition was reprinted several times before the year 1700. It was this latter which was given as Dryden's rendering in the Furness Variorum Shakespeare and in practically all collected editions of Dryden's works. Some years ago, however, Mr. W. J. Lawrence discovered that this second *Tempest*, although it has the basis of the 1670 edition, has many variations and additions, and by a nice little chain of evidence was able to state definitely that the 1674 rendering was not Dryden's comedy at all, but Shadwell's 'opera' as acted at Dorset Garden Theatre in 1674. Now, the interesting point is that this discovery, as *The Cambridge History of English Literature* points out, has not so far been introduced into the ordinary bibliographies of Dryden, and moreover, that until the volume of *Restoration Adaptations*, issued recently, Dryden's *Tempest* has never been reprinted. It was issued in 1670, now a comparatively rare quarto: it was printed in the 1701 folio edition of Dryden's works: and Professor Saintsbury noted some, not all, as Mr. Lawrence states, of its readings in his revised edition of Scott's 'Dryden.' The fact remains that up to the present year, unless we were able to secure comparatively rare original editions, possible only in the larger libraries, we could not come to any decision concerning the re-working, by the greatest writer of the last quarter of the seventeenth century, of one of the most popular plays written by his predecessor, the greatest writer of the first quarter of the seventeenth century. Although the char-acters are mainly the same in Dryden's and in Shadwell's versions, and although many of the most reprehensible scenes occur in both, the additions which appear in the 1674 edition, as well as the omissions of original Shake-speare phrases, make a careful study of the two texts, even if for Dryden's good name alone, absolutely neces-sary. Dryden retains (in an altered form), and Shadwell omits, Antonio's speech:

'We are merely cheated of our Lives by Drunkards. This wide-chopt Rascal, would thou might'st lye drowning the long washing of ten Tides.'

followed by Gonzalo's:

'He'll be hanged yet, though every drop of water swears against it: now would I give ten thousand furlongs of Sea for one Acre of barren ground, Long-heath, Broom-furs, or anything. The wills above be done, but I would fain dye a dry death.'

Dryden retains and Shadwell omits Miranda's:

'Had I been any God of power, I would have sunk the Sea into the Earth, before it should the Vessel so have swallowed.'

Similarly Dryden retains, and Shadwell deletes, Pros-pero's very effective queries, 'Dost thou attend me, Child?' and his fine fancy, 'they hoisted us, to cry to Seas which roar'd to us: to sigh to winds, whose pity sighing back again, did seem to do us loving wrong.'

In speaking of this *Tempest* as Dryden's production we must not, of course, forget that he had a colla-borator in Sir William D'Avenant. To the latter must be ascribed the blame for discovering that the plot of

Shakespeare's play was not fanciful enough. It was he who, in Dryden's words, 'designed the counterpart to *Shakespeare's* plot, namely that of a man who had never seen a Woman : that by this means those two characters of Innocence and Love might the more illustrate and commend each other.' It was he who created a twin sister for Miranda, in order to provide a mate for this unsophisticated gentleman, who was christened Hippolito. It was he who introduced Milcha, a female sprite, companion and love of Ariel, and who, in order not to leave poor Caliban without a female complement, invented a sister for him, named after her mother, Sycorax.

Because Dryden admits so much, many critics, in an endeavour to exonerate him altogether, have declared that hardly anything of the whole production can be ascribed to him and that he was heartily ashamed of the least share he had taken in it. Now, such declarations seem to me to display a lack of acquaintanceship with the spirit of the Restoration period. There is no use glozing over the matter. We have here Dryden's express testimony that he approved of the alterations : and we have, moreover, his statement that all but the sailors' parts were written or rewritten by him alone, and merely revised or criticised by D'Avennant.

What do we find when we come to the actual development of the plot of this precious production ? We find, first of all, a vast amount of buffoonery and would-be humor put into the mouths of Trincalo, who becomes the self-styled Duke of the Island, and of his companions : and we find a mass of suggestive sentences in the scenes between Dorinda, Hippolito and Miranda. In point of fact, all the attention is deviated from Prospero, who becomes merely a lay figure, and the great bulk of the dialogue is given to the sailors, or to the group of the three innocents.

The Duke Trincalo episodes are clearly the result of

semi-political motives added to the new idea of fun. They were possibly the most popular portions of the play. Otway in the Epilogue to his *The Souldier's Fortune* (1680) addresses the poets:

> ' O Poets, have a care of one another,
>   There's hardly one amongst ye true to 'tother :
>   Like *Trincalo's* and *Stephano's* ye Play
>   The lewdest Tricks, each other to betray,'

while Settle, in the dedication to his *The Distress'd Innocence* (1690) has a bye-reference to Trincalo and his Dukedom, which shows that it was still popular more than twenty years after its first production.

The other scenes of suggestive innocence are as obviously the result of the immoral, degenerate qualities of the age. The Restoration liked such scenes. It loved to hear the coarsest of sentiments retailed by girls hardly out of their teens, and there are several plays, such as Mrs. Behn's *The Young King: or, The Mistake*, where we find boys and maidens who have mysteriously been kept from all human intercourse, and who speak with a freedom born of ignorance and of licentious instinct. In these scenes, all Shakespeare's modesty and reserve are gone : Dorinda and Miranda, observes Scott, talk ' the language of prostitution before' they ' ever have seen a man,' and Hippolito, reared in seclusion, utters the sentiments of the most gay and reckless roué of Congreve or of Etherege.

As might be expected, with all these domestic complications of Prospero, those scenes which preserve some of their Shakespearian phrasing become at times almost ludicrous.

> ' I have done nothing but in care of thee,
>   My daughter, and thy pretty sister,'

Prospero is forced to declare : and again,

> ' Thy Mother was all Virtue, and she said, thou wast my Daughter, and thy Sister too.'

Still again :

'On a night
  Mated to his Design, Antonio opened the Gates of Millan,
  and i' the dead of darkness, hurri'd me thence with thy young
    Sister, and thy crying self.'

And yet again :

'Thou and thy Sister were two Cherubins, which did preserve me: you both did smile, infus'd with fortitude from
Heaven.'

Such was Shakespeare's fate in the year 1667. So
popular was this wondrous adaptation that Anthony à
Wood, chronicling *The Tempest*, had no hesitation in
writing down that 'This Play was originally Shakespeare's.' Hippolito and Dorinda it took many a year
to drive from the English stage.

When we turn to observe this *Tempest* from that other
aspect which we proposed to ourselves at the beginning
of this paper, we are met with a difficulty. In places
Dryden evidently follows F1 : for example, in I ii, l. 288,
he has 'what' whereas the other Ff have 'which.' In
other places, however, he seems to have gone directly
to one of the other Ff: for example in I ii, l. 517, where
F1 has 'ungently' while the other Ff and Dryden have
'urgently.' In still other places he appears to agree
with neither. The most interesting example of this
last occurs in the speech beginning 'Abhorr'd Slave!'
which was given in all the Ff to Miranda. It appears
first ascribed to Prospero in Dryden, and all editors of
Shakespeare have agreed with him in the ascription.

Duffett's *The Mock-Tempest: or, The Enchanted Castle*
(Theatre Royal, 1674), was not an 'adaptation' of
Shakespeare, but a burlesque of Shadwell's opera as
presented at the rival theatre at Dorset Garden earlier
in the same year. Among the characters are '*Prospero*
—a Duke, Head-Keeper of the Enchanted Castle,':

'*Hypolito*—infant Duke of *Mantua*, Innocent and Ignorant,': '*Miranda* and *Dorinda*—harmless Daughters of Prospero.' The scene is carried to London, and many of the scenes take place in the 'Enchanted Castle,'— which is Bridewell. Although Dryden's pair of innocents are moderately well ticked off, there is little of wit or brilliancy in this crude piece of Restoration vulgarity, and it has very little to do with Shakespeare. The following brief abstraɕt may give some idea of its tenor:

Prosp. *Miranda*, you must now leave this Tom-rigging, and learn to behave yourself with a grandeur and state, befit-ting your illustrious Birth and Quality.—Thy Father, *Miranda*, was 50 years ago a man of great power, Duke of my Lord Mayor's Dog-Kennel.

Mir. O lo, why Father, Father, are not I *Miranda Whiffe*, Sooth, and arn't you *Prospero Whiffe*, Sooth, Keeper of *Bride-well*, my Father?

Prosp. Thy Mother was all Mettle, as true as Steel, and she said thou wert my Daughter; canst thou remember when thou wert born, sure thou canst not, for then thou wert but three days old.

Mir. I'fads, I do remember it, Father, as well as 'twere but yesterday.

And so on: but not always in so delicate a strain. Ariel is given a terminal song:

> Where good Ale is, there suck I,
> In a Cobler's stall I lye,
> While the Watch is passing by;
> Then about the streets I fly,
> After Cullies merrily. . . .

Dryden's second alteration of a Shakespearian drama was the famous *All for Love: or, The World Well Lost* aɕted at Drury Lane in 1677. This was the play, which not only was best loved by its own author, but, apparently, came to be regarded as a kind of symbol of his highest art. In a broadside called *The Patentee*, printed in 1700, the theatre is apostrophised:

> Ah! see the Place where thy *Ventidius* stood,
> Bending with years, and most profusely good,
> Unmov'd by Fate, and of unshaken Truth,
> His Counsels those of Age, his Courage that of Youth:
> Where mourning *Anthony* contesting strove
> Which to relinquish, Honour, or his Love,
> As ev'ry Hearer's Sorrows took his Part,
> And truly wept for him who griev'd with Art.

The reference here to the struggle between Love and Honor serves to delineate one of the reasons for the popularity of the play. *All for Love* came just when rhymed was giving way to blank verse, and when classicism was tempering a trifle the rather bombastic scenes of the heroic tragedy proper. *All for Love* is a classicised specimen of the heroic school. 'The Unities of Time, Place and Action,' Dryden tells us, are 'more exactly observ'd, than perhaps the *English* Theatre requires.' The mighty and ultra-romantic changes from Rome to Alexandria and back again, which are so characteristic of Shakespeare's *Anthony*, are reduced practically to one single scene: the time is one day: the passions are simplified, and the scenes clear and developed. Not that Dryden has made a complete submission to the French school. French 'Heroes' he tells us, 'are the most Civil People breathing, but their good Breeding seldom extends to a word of Sense: All their Wit is in their Ceremony: they want the Genius which animates our Stage' and the whole play, in his own words, is avowedly 'Written in Imitation of *Shakespeare's* Style.'

The five acts of *All for Love* are clean cut as five separate cameos. In the first Ventidius reproaches Anthony and weans him from Cleopatra. In the second we find Cleopatra in despair: she meets Anthony, who

spurns her, but is in the end won back to her love.
In the third, we find Anthony and Cleopatra together;
Octavia arrives and Anthony is again won back for
Rome: at the close Octavia and Cleopatra have a little
word duel in Restoration style.   We can imagine Nell
Gwyn and some other Court favourite quarrelling over
Charles in the same way.   In the fourth act, Anthony
sends Dolabella to Cleopatra.   Dolabella falls in love
with her, and is almost false when honor triumphs in
his breast.   Anthony is jealous, and Octavia, realising
that she has lost him again, departs.   In the fifth we
hear of the treachery of the Egyptian fleet, and Anthony
believes that Cleopatra has been false.   Cleopatra retires
to a monument and Alexas announces treacherously to
Anthony that she has killed herself.   Anthony and
Ventidius commit suicide.   Cleopatra enters to find the
former dying and applies the asp to her arm.

Much more than in Shakespeare we feel here the
battledore and shuttlecock movement of Anthony's
emotions: and we seem to feel, although not in so great
a measure as is often made out, the conflict, not between
love for Cleopatra and a ' Roman thought,' but between
love for Cleopatra and duty as expressed in Octavia.
Anthony has many of the characteristics of Almanzor,
with the same prowess, the same psychology that seems
to see no more than two emotions, Love and Honor,
the same preternatural nobility.   Like Anthony, Cleopatra is a being of simple feelings, a sister of the true
heroic heroine, and Dolabella, with a like contest in his
heart, is the typical hero's friend, reproducing his emo-
tion.   We may well criticise Dryden's play from the
standpoint of psychological description when we com-
pare it with Shakespeare's *Anthony*: and yet, however
we may criticise, it remains a great drama.   It is far
more a suggested than an adapted play, and, after *Venice
Preserv'd*, is, undoubtedly, the finest of the Restoration,
we might almost say, late Elizabethan, tragedies.

Troilus and Cressida, acted in 1679, Dryden's third adaptation from Shakespeare, presents no interesting features as regards the mere text, as Dryden himself informs us that he took it from one of the Folios. It does, however, raise some valuable points in the question of critical and other changes in the development of Shakespeare's plot. Dryden himself, in his preface, after remarking on Shakespeare's greatness, and stating that ' our Reverence for *Shakespear* (is) much more just, than that of the *Grecians* for *Aeschylus*,' raises four objections to the earlier *Troilus*. First, he says, echoing the words of his contemporaries, much of the language is obsolete, ungrammatical, coarse and too figurative. Secondly, the play has not been divided into acts and scenes, and the whole moves with a careless, incoherent motion. Thirdly, ' the latter part of the Tragedy is nothing but a confusion of Drums and Trumpets, Excursions and Alarms '—the words are Dryden's own. On turning to his own adaptation, one might think that he has increased the fighting and this 'Confusion of Excursions and Alarms '—but Dryden's criticism is directed rather at what seemed to him the *purposeless* confusion than at the confusion itself. Finally, as a fourth objection, Dryden finds that ' the chief Persons . . . are left alive : *Cressida* is false, and is not punish'd.'

On looking at Dryden's adaptation, the first thing that we notice is that he has made the various short and shifting scenes more coherent. He has not, naturally, been able to keep a strict unity of place, but at least he has been able to link together a number of Troy scenes, and then a number of Greek scenes, so as to avoid an incessant ebb and flow of location. This, however, is not the main point in his alteration. At first sight, we would have thought that Shakespeare's *Troilus and Cressida*, with its satirical bent, and its vision of weak women and vainglorious men, would not have appealed to the Restoration consciousness, and

Dryden knew that, as it stood, it would not appeal. He has, therefore, sharply divided the play into tragedy and comedy. He has made nearly all the Grecian and Trojan warriors 'heroes': he has ennobled Troilus and has kept Cressida pure and true as a tragic heroine ought to be. To achieve this, of course, not only had many Shakespearian scenes to be omitted, but practically the whole of the fifth act had to be written anew. In Dryden's version, Cressida, after she had left the town of Troy, yearns for Troilus, but Calchas, pointing out to her that Diomede is their only friend among the Greeks, and that he himself has 'a Woman's Longing to return' to Troy, bids her pretend love to Diomede and give him the ring of Troilus. As in Shakespeare, Ulysses and Troilus, with Thersites apart, hear the love scene, which in this case, of course, is feigned, as Cressida tells us in asides. Later on, Troilus bursts in pursuing Diomede, but Cressida, for her father's sake, begs him to spare the latter's life. Troilus reproaches her, and she, stung by his taunts, commits suicide. Thereupon a general fight ensues wherein Troilus slays Diomede, and then is himself overpowered by superior numbers. This dénouement explains the second title to Dryden's play—*Troilus and Cressida: or, Truth found too Late.*

As an undercurrent to this tragic and almost heroic plot go the Pandarus and Thersites scenes, which are considerably elaborated. It was this elaborated Pandarus which probably gave a hint to Otway for his Sir Jolly Jumble in *The Souldier's Fortune* (Dorset Garden, 1680). These scenes, along with a lengthy passage in the third act, between Troilus and Hector, admittedly imitated from *Julius Cæsar* and the *Iphigenia* of Euripides, make up for the omissions of unheroic sentiments among the warriors of Greece. Here, again, then, we see the same phenomenon—the making more heroic of serious sentiments and characters, and the debasing and vulgarising of comic situations.

In *Troilus and Cressida*, still further, we find an example of other changes due to the political tendency in the contemporary drama. In Shakespeare Calchas is a priest and nothing more. In Dryden—for Dryden was then in an anti-priest mood—Calchas and all priests are cursed and ridiculed out of existence. 'And will you promise that the holy Priest shall make us one for ever?' asks Cressida, to which comes Pandarus' answer straight, 'Priests marry, hang 'em!' Cressida, we are told, has run 'to the fugitive rogue Priest her father.' 'That I shou'd trust the Daughter of a Priest!' muses Troilus:

> 'Priesthood, that makes a Merchandise of Heaven!
> Priesthood, that sells ev'n to their Pray'rs and Blessings!
> And forces us to pay for our own Coz'nage.'

To which Thersites chimes in:

> 'Nay, cheats Heav'n too with Entrails and with Offals:
> Give it the Garbage of a Sacrifice,
> And keeps the best for private Luxury.'

whereupon Troilus tells him:

> 'Thou hast deserv'd thy Life for cursing Priests.'

This note runs all through the play, as does the note in favor of royal supremacy.

'When Supremacy of Kings is shaken,' Dryden asks in the first act, 'What can succeed?' and he closes on a note familiar to all students of the Restoration drama, with a curse on 'those thought Patriots' and on 'factious Nobles':

> 'Then since from home-bred Faction Ruin springs,
> Let Subjects learn Obedience to their Kings!'

Troilus and Cressida is Dryden's last definite alteration of Shakespeare, although I must just mention in passing an adaptation of *Julius Cæsar* which appeared in 1719. The title page informs us that it was 'alter'd by Sir

William D'Avenant and *John Dryden.*' Let us hope it
was not. At any rate there is nothing whatever to show
that the ascription first made here was justified. *Julius
Cæsar* was printed several times during the late seventeenth century, with a few minor changes, and, although
those changes were retained in the 1719 edition, there
do not appear in the earlier copies the additional scenes
and couplets which, whenever they were added, seem
to have persisted in acting versions of *Julius Cæsar*
until the end of the eighteenth century. One of the
priceless passages occurs at the close of the fourth act,
where Brutus after seeing the ghost thus communes with
himself:

> ' Sure they have rais'd some Devil to their Aid,
> And think to frighten *Brutus* with a Shade.
> But ere the Night closes this fatal Day,
> I'll send more Ghosts this visit to repay.'

Brutus, however, is not able to pay his party call, or
get any supernatural agent to do it for him, and Cæsar's
ghost returns at the field of Philippi. ' Next, ungrateful *Brutus*,' it cries. ' do I call. ' Ungrateful *Cæsar*,'
answers Brutus, ' that wou'd *Rome* enthral.' To which
the ghost, 'The *Ides* of *March*, remember—I must go.'
It sinks down—the stage direction informs us. One
would have enjoyed, just for once, hearing those lines
seriously uttered on the stage !

Whether I have been successful I know not, but I
have endeavoured, in this very brief compass, to bring
to the surface some of what appear to me the more
interesting characteristics of this study of Shakespeare
in an altered dress. We cannot forget when we are
dealing with these early adaptations that we are con-
nected on the one hand, through Davenant, with earlier
theatrical tradition and with Shakespeare himself, on the
other, through Dryden and his companion poets, with
the very temper and deepest artistic feelings of the ages
which have gone before us.

A BRIEF BIBLIOGRAPHY OF SHAKESPEARE
ADAPTATIONS, 1660-1700

[Including editions of plays printed between 1660 and 1700,
and indicating dates of performance where ascertainable.
'L.C.' papers refers to documents in the Public Record
Office, Lord Chamberlain's department.]

1. *The Tempest.*

The Tempest, or the Enchanted Island. A Comedy.
As it is now Acted at his Highness the Duke of York's
Theatre . . . [*Henry Herringman.*] MDCLXX.

> [Two issues, preface signed by Dryden: reprinted in the
> 1701 *Works* of Dryden. Pepys witnessed this at the
> Lincoln's Inn Fields Theatre on Thur., 7 Nov., Wed. 13
> Nov., and Thur., 12 Dec., 1667: on Mon., 6 Jan., Mon.,
> 3 Feb., Thur., 30 April, and Mon., 11 May, 1668: and
> on Thur., 21 Jan., 1669. In the L.C. records there are
> references to other performances on Thur., 14 and Tu.,
> 26 Nov., 1667: Sat., 14 Mar., 1667/8, and Mon., 13
> April, 1668. Downes, *Roscius Anglicanus*, p. 33.]

The Tempest, or the Enchanted Island. A Comedy
. . . (as above) [*Henry Herringman.*] MDCLXXIV.

> [This retains Dryden's preface, but is the 'opera' made
> by Shadwell from the Dryden-D'Avenant alteration of
> 1670. Later editions followed in 1676 (*bis*), 1690, 1701.
> All editions of Dryden's works after that of 1701 give
> this text. This opera appeared at the Dorset Garden in
> 1674 with a special prologue (B.M. MS. Eg. 2623: see
> Downes, p. 34). It was burlesqued by Duffett in his The
> Mock-Tempest: or the Enchanted Castle. Acted at the
> Theatre Royal . . . 1675. This appeared in Nov., 1674.
> References are to be found in the L.C. papers to per-
> formances of *The Tempest* opera on Tu., 17, Wed. 18, and
> Sat., 28 Nov., 1674, and Thur., 15 Nov., 1677.]

2. *The Merry Wives of Windsor.*

[Played at the Red Bull (Herbert records) and at the first Theatre Royal on Friday, 9 Nov., 1660 (Herbert). Pepys saw it on Wed., 5 Dec., 1660, Wed., 25th Sept., 1661, and Thur., 15 Aug., 1667. A performance of this play is recorded in the L.C. papers on Fri., 17 Dec., 1675. No printed version of the text used is extant.]

3. *Measure for Measure.*

The Law against Lovers [printed first in D'Avenant's Works, 1673].

[This is a free alteration of *Measure for Measure* with the addition of the Benedick scenes of *Much Ado.* Pepys saw it at the Lincoln's Inn Fields Theatre on Tuesday, 18 Feb., 1661/2: it was presented at Court on Wed., 17 Dec. of that year (Evelyn). See Downes, p. 26.]

Measure for Measure, or Beauty the Best Advocate. As it is Acted At the Theatre in Lincolns-Inn-Fields. Written Originally by Mr. Shakespeare: And now very much Alter'd; With Additions of Several Entertainments of Musick . . . [*D. Brown* and *R. Parker.*] 1700.

[This was acted at the new Lincoln's Inn Fields house probably in 1699 or in 1700. It is the work of Charles Gildon.]

4. *A Midsummer-Night's Dream.*

The Fairy-Queen: an Opera. Represented at the Queen's Theatre By Their Majesties Servants . . . [*Jacob Tonson.*] 1692.

[The author of this opera is not known, although Settle has been suggested. It was entered in the Stationers' Register for 2 Nov., 1691 (Roxburghe Edition III. 393) and in 1693 was reprinted 'With Alterations, Additions and Several New Songs.' It was originally acted at the Dorset Garden Theatre probably about October, 1691. A performance, probably with the 'Alterations,' is recorded for Tu., 16 Feb., 1691/2 (L.C.). *A Midsummer-*

Night's Dream, probably unaltered, was seen by Pepys at the Theatre Royal on Mon., 29 Sept., 1662.]

5. *The Taming of the Shrew.*

Sauny the Scott: or, the Taming of the Shrew: A Comedy. As it is now Acted at the Theatre-Royal. Written by J. Lacey, Servant to His Majesty. And Never before printed. *Then I'll cry out, Swell'd with Poetic Rage, 'Tis I,* John Lacey, *have Reform'd your Stage.* Prol. *to* Rehers . . . [*E. Whitlock.*] 1698.

[This was probably the alteration Pepys saw on Tuesday, 9 April, 1667, and on Fri., 1 Nov., 1667. *The Taming of the Shrew,* no doubt unaltered, had already been acted in 1663.]

6. *Twelfth Night.*

[*Twelfth Night* was acted at Lincoln's Inn Fields Theatre on Wed., 11 Sept., 1661, Tu., 6 Jan., 1662/3, and Wed., 20 Jan., 1668/9 (Pepys). See Downes, p. 22.]

B. *HISTORIES*

1. *Henry IV.*

K. Henry IV. with the humours of Sir John Falstaff. A Tragi-Comedy. As it is Acted at the Theatre in Little-Lincolns-Inn-Fields by His Majesty's Servants. Revived, with Alterations. Written Originally by Mr. Shakespear . . . [*R. W.* and Sold by *John Deeve.*] 1700.

[*Henry IV* was given by Herbert as an original Red Bull play: it was the play with which the first Theatre Royal opened on Thur., 8 Nov., 1660. Pepys saw it on Mon., 31 Dec., 1660, and on Tu., 4 June, 1661. Later he was at productions of it on Sat., 2 Nov., 1667, Tu., 7 Jan., and Fri., 18 Sept., 1668. See Downes, p. 7. The alteration given above has been attributed to Betterton, and, if his, must have come out after 1695 (the opening of the new Lincoln's Inn Fields Theatre).]

2. *Henry VI.*

The Misery of Civil War. A Tragedy, As it is Acted at the Duke's Theatre, By His Royal Highnesses Servants. Written by Mr. Crown . . . [*R. Bentley* and *M. Magnes.*] 1680. Reissued as Henry the Sixth, The Second Part. Or the Misery of Civil War . . . 1681.

Henry the Sixth, The First Part. With the Murder of Humphrey, Duke of Glocester. As it was Acted at the Duke's Theatre. Written by Mr. Crown . . . [*R. Bentley* and *M. Magnes.*] 1681.

[*The Misery of Civil War* was entered in *The Term Catalogues* in May, 1680 (ed. Arber I. 394); the reissue in Nov., 1681 (I. 462). It had been acted at Dorset Garden Theatre probably early in 1680. *Henry the Sixth* was entered in Nov., 1681 (I. 462) and was acted at the same theatre probably in the summer of 1681.]

3. *Henry VIII.*

[*Henry VIII*, probably in an altered form, was produced with ornate settings in December, 1663. Pepys saw it on Friday, 1 Jan., 1663/4, and later on Wed., 30 Dec., 1668. This play was seen by the King later on Tu., 3 Sept., 1672. See Downes, p. 24.]

4. *Richard II.*

The History of King Richard The Second. Acted at the Theatre Royal, under the Name of the Sicilian Usurper. With a Prefatory *Epistle* in Vindication of the Author. Occasion'd by the Prohibition of this Play on the Stage. By N. Tate. *Inultus ut Flebo Puer?* Hor. . . . [*Richard Tonson* and *Jacob Tonson.*] 1681.

[Entered in the Term Catalogues, June, 1681 (I. 451) and, as the warrant ordering its suppression appears in the L.C. records dated 14 Dec., 1680, acted probably in the winter of 1680. It was reprinted in 1691 as *The Sicilian Usurper.*]

5. *Richard III.*

The Tragical History of King Richard III. As it is Acted at the Theatre Royal. By C. Cibber.——Domestica Facta . . . [*B. Lintott* and *A. Bettesworth.*] 1700.

> [Undated but entered in the Term Catalogues, Feb., 1700 (III. 173). Acted at Drury Lane probably towards the close of 1699.]

C. TRAGEDIES

1. *Troilus and Cressida.*

Troilus and Cressida, or, Truth Found too Late. A Tragedy As it is Acted at the Duke's Theatre. To which is Prefix'd, A Preface Containing the Grounds of Criticism in Tragedy. Written by John Dryden Servant to his Majesty. *Rectius, Iliacum carmen deducis in actus. Quam si proferres ignota indictaque primus.* Hor. . . . [*Jacob Tonson* and *Abel Small.*] 1679.

> [Entered in the Stationers' Register, 14 April, 1679 (III. 83): in the Term Catalogues, Nov., 1679 (I. 370) and acted at Dorset Garden about March, 1679.]

2. *Coriolanus.*

The Ingratitude of a Common-wealth: or, the Fall of Caius Martius Coriolanus. As it is Acted at the Theatre-Royal. By N. Tate. *Honoratum si forte reponis Achillem, Impiger, Iracundus, Inexorabilis, Acer, Jura neget sibi nata, nihil non arroget Armis.* Hor. . . . [*Joseph Hindmarsh.*] 1682.

> [Entered in the Term Catalogues, Feb., 1682 (I. 473), and acted at Drury Lane probably late in 1681.]

3. *Titus Andronicus.*

Titus Andronicus, or the Rape of Lavinia. Acted at the Theatre Royall, A Tragedy, Alter'd from Mr. Shakespears Works, By Mr. Edw. Ravenscroft. Licensed, Dec. 21. 1686. R.L.S. . . . [*J. Hindmarsh.*] 1687.

[Entered in the Term Catalogues, Feb., 1687 (II. 188) and acted at D. L. probably in 1678. Downes (p. 8) mentions *Titus Andronicus* among the plays acted by the King's Company at the Theatre Royal in Vere Street.]

4. *Romeo and Juliet.*

The History and Fall of Caius Marius. A Tragedy. As it is Aćted at the Duke's Theatre. By Thomas Otway. *Qui color Albus erat nunc est contrarius Albo.* . . . [*Tho. Flesher.*] 1680.

[Entered in the Term Catalogues, Nov., 1679 (I. 370) and acted at Dorset Garden Theatre probably in October, 1679. It was reprinted in 1692, 1694 and 1696. Downes (p. 22) notes a tragi-comedy made out of *Romeo* by Howard and performed alternately with the Shakespeare original. This version is lost. Pepys saw *Romeo* on Sat., 1 March, 1662 at the Lincoln's Inn Fields Theatre.]

5. *Timon of Athens.*

The History of Timon of Athens, The Man-Hater. As it is aćted at the Duke's Theatre. Made into a Play. By Tho. Shadwell. Licensed, *Feb.* 18. 167$\frac{8}{7}$. *Ro. L'Estrange* . . . [*Henry Herringman.*] 1678.

[Entered in the Stationers' Register 23 Feb., 1677/8 (III. 58). It was reprinted in 1680 (Term Catalogues, Dec., 1680, II. 240), 1688, 1696 and 1703. The production in the Dorset Garden Theatre was probably in Jan., 1677/8.]

6. *Julius Cæsar.*

Julius Cæsar. A Tragedy. As it is now Aćted at the Theatre Royal. Written by William Shakespeare . . . [*Hen. Herringman* and *R. Bentley.*] 1684.

[There are at least three other undated quarto issues and one dated 1691. See 'THE LIBRARY' for 1913, article by Henrietta C. Bartlett. Genest thinks a revival had already

taken place in 1671 (see Downes, p. 8). A later alteration appeared in vol. i of A Collection of Play By Eminent
Hands . . . MDCCXIX, there attributed to Dryden and
D'Avenant. *Julius Cæsar* as printed in 1684 was seen by
the King on Mon., 4 Dec., 1676, and at Court on Mon.,
18 April, 1687 (L.C. Records.)]

7. *Macbeth*.

Macbeth, A Tragedy. Acted At the Dukes-Theatre
. . . [*William Cademan.*]   1673.

Macbeth, a Tragœdy. With all the Alterations,
Amendments, Additions, and New Songs. As it's now
Acted at the Dukes Theatre . . . [*P. Chetwin.*]   1674.

[See Term Catalogues, May, 1673 (I. 134) and July, 1674
(l. 179) Herbert notes a revival of *Macbeth* in Nov.,
1663, and Pepys saw it at Lincoln's Inn Fields on Sat.,
5 Nov., 1664. No doubt this was the play as given in
the 1673 quarto, which Pepys saw later on Fri., 28 Dec.,
1666, Mon., 7 Jan., Fri., 19 April, Wed., 16 Oct., and
Wed., 6 Nov., 1667, Wed., 12 Aug., and Mon., 21 Dec.,
1668, and Fri., 15 Jan., 1669. A performance of this play
at Court was given on Mon., 17 Dec., 1666. The 1674
quarto (reprinted 1687, 1697 and 1710), probably a re-
alteration by D'Avenant, is referred to by Downes (p. 33)
as a revival 'being in the nature of an opera.' There is
a record of a performance of this *Macbeth* (L.C. papers)
on Tu., 18 Feb., 1672/3 ; this may well be the first night
of production. The play was revived later on Mon., 8
Feb., 1685/6.]

8. *Hamlet*.

The Tragedy of Hamlet Prince of Denmark. As it
is now Acted at his Highness the Duke of York's
Theatre. By William Shakespeare . . . [*J. Martyn* and
H. Herringman.]   1676.

[Another edition appeared the same year for the same
publishers. It was reprinted in 1683 ; and again in 1695
'As it is now Acted at the Theatre Royal.' The lines cut are

marked by inverted commas. *Hamlet* was seen by **Pepys** at the Lincoln's Inn Fields Theatre on Sat., 24 Aug., Wed., 27 Nov., and Thur., 5 Dec., 1661, and Thur., 28 May, 1663, by Evelyn on Tu., 26 Nov., 1661. Pepys went to a performance later on Mon., 31 Aug., 1668. The King was present at performances of this play on Wed., 2 Dec., 1674, and Fri., 30 April, 1686. See Downes, p. 20.]

9. *Lear.*

The History of King Lear. Acted at the Duke's Theatre. Reviv'd with Alterations. By **N**. Tate . . . [*E. Flesher.*] 1681.

[*Lear* according to Downes (p. 26) had been early played at Lincoln's Inn Fields Theatre. This adaptation of Tate's (entered in the **Term** Catalogues, May, 1681, I. 440, and reprinted 1689, 1699, 1703 and 1712) was acted at Dorset Garden probably about Jan., 1681. This was the version that the King witnessed on Mon., 9 May, 1687, and on Mon., 20 Feb., 1687/8.]

10. *Othello.*

Othello, The Moor of Venice. A Tragedy. As it hath been divers times Acted at the Globe, and at the Black-Friers: And now at the Theatre Royal, By His Majesties Servants. Written by William Shakespear . . . [*W. Weak.*] 1681.

[*Othello* was played at the Red Bull, and at the first Theatre Royal on Sat., 8 Dec., 1660 (Herbert). It was acted at Court on 11 Oct., 1660 (Pepys) and at the Theatre Royal on Sat., 6 Feb., 1668/9. See Downes, p. 6 and p. 40 when he chronicles a revival after the Union of the Companies in 1682. Reprints appeared in 1687, 1695, and 1705. From the L.C. records there seems to have been a special revival on Mon., 25 Jan., 1674-5, another on Wed., 12 Jan., 1675/6, and another (no doubt the revival chronicled by Downes) on Fri., 18 Jan., 1683/4. *Othello* was later played at Drury Lane on Sat., 30 May, 1685, at Court on Tu., 24 Nov., 1685, and Wed., 10 Nov., 1686.]

11. *Antony and Cleopatra.*

All for Love or, The World Well Lost.   A Tragedy,
As it is Acted at the Theatre-Royal; And Written in
Imitation of Shakespeare's Stile.   By John Dryden,
Servant to His Majesty.   *Facile est verbum aliquod ardens
(ut ita dicam) notare; idque restinctis animorum incendiis
irridere.*   Cicero . . . [*Henry Herringman.*]   1678.

> [Reprinted 1692: 1696: 1703: 1709: 1711 and in
> editions of Dryden's works.   Entered in the Stationers'
> Register for 31 Jan., 1677/8 (III. 56) and acted at Drury
> Lane probably late in 1677.   The first performance may
> have taken place on Wed., 12 Dec. of that year.   It was
> revived later on Wed., 20 Jan., 1685/6, at Court (L.C.
> Records].   Sedley's *Antony and Cleopatra* (not an alteration
> of Shakespeare) was produced at Dorset Garden on Mon.,
> 12 Feb., 1676/7 (L.C. Records).]

12. *Pericles.*

> [Downes (p. 18) marks *Pericles* as having been acted at
> the Cockpit.]

13. *Cymbeline.*

The Injured Princess, or the Fatal VVager : As it was
Acted at the Theater-Royal, By His Majesties Servants.
By Tho. Durfey, Gent . . . [*R. Bentley* and *M. Magnes.*]
1682.

> [Entered in the Term Catalogues, May, 1682 (I. 485)
> and Nov., 1682 (I. 509) and acted at Drury Lane prob-
> ably about Jan., 1682.]

NOTE

By Lord Chamberlain's warrant most of the Elizabethan plays (including Shakespeare's) were made the exclusive property of one or other of the two theatres in Restoration times. R. W. Lowe discovered the first of these warrants, that dated 12th December, 1660, by which D'Avenant was given the right of performing and 'making fitt' nine plays of Shakespeare 'the Tempest, Measures for Measures, Much adoe about nothinge, Rome and Juliet, Twelfe night, the Life of Kinge Henry the Eyght, Kinge Lear, the Tragedy of Macbeth, the Tragedy of Hamlet prince of Denmarke,' and also the right of playing for two months from the date of warrant 'Persiles prince of Tyre.'

Lowe, however, appears to have missed two later documents which I have discovered while searching through the Lord Chamberlain's papers for material which I have utilised in a forthcoming *History of Restoration Drama*. The first of these is twice entered, once in the Warrant Book L.C. 5/139 p. 375, and again in the Warrant Book L.C. 5/12 p. 209. This, which is dated 20th August, 1668, gives some 23 'playes allowed to be acted by his Royall Highnesse ye Duke of Yorkes Comœdians' and includes three plays of Shakespeare, 'Timon of Athens, Troyolus and Crisseida, Three parts of H : ye 6:' The second warrant is undated (it appears in L.C. 5/12 p. 212) but it occurs among other documents of about 12th January, 1668/9, and evidently corresponds to the grant given to the Duke's company. It gives 'A Catalogue of Part of his Ma^{tes} Servants Playes as they were formerley acted at the Blackfryars & now allowed of to his Ma^{tes} Servants at ye New Theatre.' It is a lengthy list and includes nearly all the Shakespeare plays not given to D'Avenant:—'The Winter's Tale, King John, Richard the Second, The Gentlemen of Verona, The Merry Wives of Windsor, The Comœdy of Errors, Loves Labour Lost, Midsomer Nights Dreame, The Merchant of Venice, As you like it, The Taming of y^e Shrew, Alls Well y^t ends well, Henry y^e fourth, The second part (of the same), Richard y^e Third, Coriolanus, Andronicus, Julius Ceaser, The Moore of Venice, Anthony & Cleopatra, Cymbelyne.'